A BASIC MIDDLE EASTERN DESERT SURVIVAL GUIDE

OF COMMON EDIBLE WILD FOODS

Environmentarian movement: Linda Runyon

A BASIC MIDDLE EASTERN DESERT SURVIVAL GUIDE

OF COMMON WILD FOODS

Lamb's Quarters
Chenopodium species
'Aifajan

Kurdish Studies

The International Journal

The Kurdish Library

Volume 5, Numbers 1 & 2
Spring–Fall 1992

Additions have been added to the original 5,000 word manuscript.

The plants themselves are found throughout the entire Middle East.

Happy FORAGING!!!

Please note: The following introduction "Common Edible Wild Plants of Kurdistan" was written for the original Kurdish Studies. Note also: The plant information pertains to the entire Middle East.

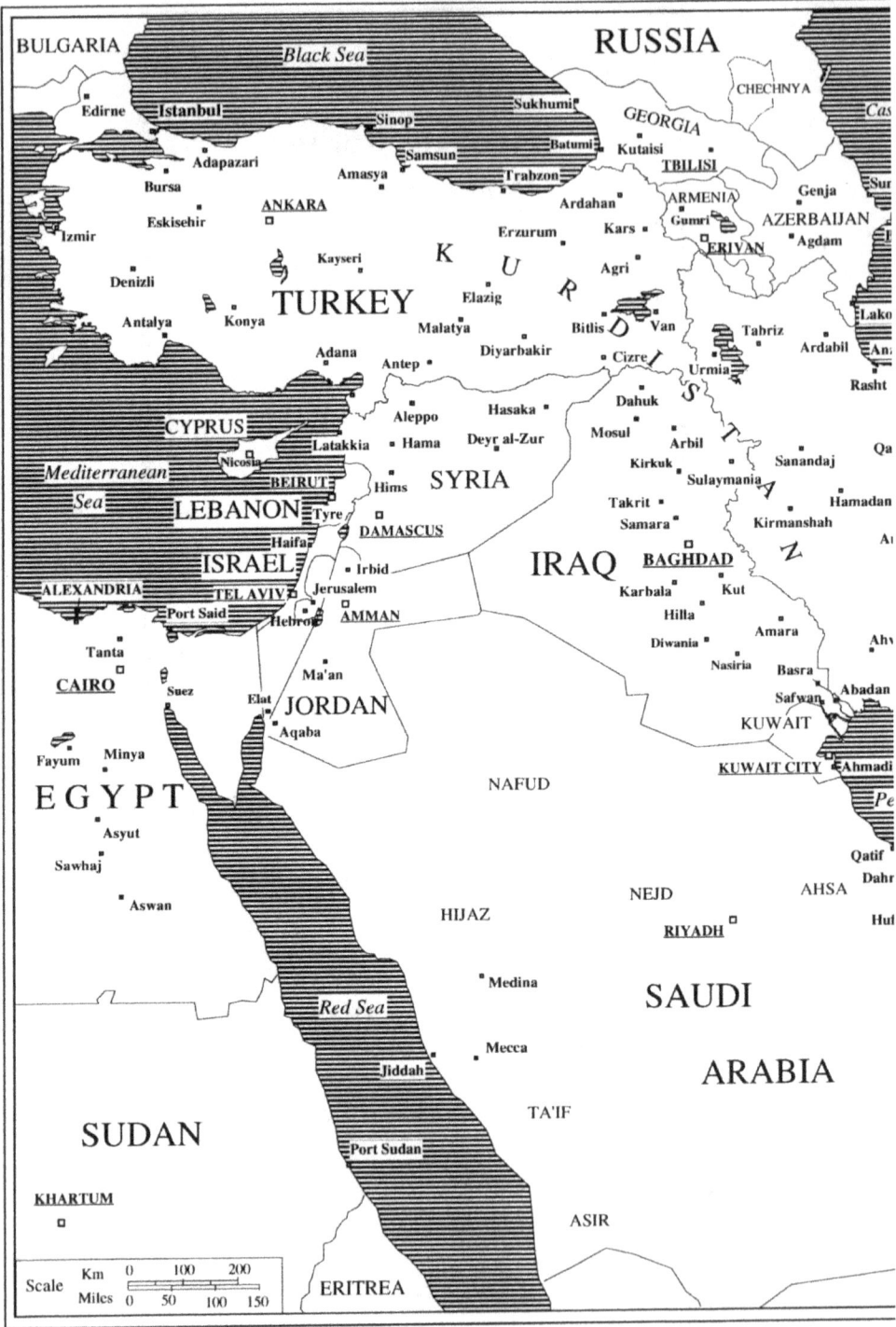

MAP OF THE MIDDLE EAST, FEBRUARY 1997

iv

Map 1. Greater Middle East: Countries and Regions.

EGYPT	Country	■ Herat	City
KURDISTAN	Region	□ DUSHANBE	Capital city

MAP OF THE MIDDLE EAST, FEBRUARY 1997

TABLE OF CONTENTS

COMMON EDIBLE WILD PLANTS OF KURDISTAN

Linda Runyon

The Kurdish Highlands are widely believed from archaeological evidence to have been the source of a very large number of our domesticated common plant and animal foods. Of plants, we need only to mention wheat, barley, oat, lentils, peas and grapes to realize the magnitude of our debt to the ancestors of the Kurds who domesticated and passed on to the rest of humanity what is now the staff of life for a majority of people living today. Wild ancestors of these plants are still found widespread across the Zagros and Taurus Mountains in Kurdistan. In fact, three of these early domesticates—chickweed, wild oat, and plantain—appear here in the survey. Other, lesser-known edible plants that abound in Kurdish countryside have not been utilized as a human food source, and remain in their pristine state.

Over the ages, our civilizations have organized and grouped our food. They have been hybridized, altered, and prepared in hundreds of practical ways. We, as a race of civilized people, have sprayed pesticides and herbicides, and have poisoned, burned, and discarded, the hated "weed". While millions go hungry, this wild food has continued to be present in abundance and has always been mutely accessible as food source to all. Kurdish highlands are no exception to this natural abundance. Wild plants and their utility remain unknown to most present-day refugees and even those on extended expeditions through wilderness.

Many of these plants surveyed here also have medicinal and hygienic uses in addition to being edible. I strongly suggest making note of these additional benefits that might well come in handy in emergencies especially in the inaccessible parts of Kurdish mountains. Plantain leaves, for example, can serve as antiseptic bandage, the juice of sorrel helps skin irritation from eruptions, while the roots of wild spinach can be used as a soap substitute.

It should be noted that most plants mentioned here appear in creek bottoms, irrigated areas, as well as mountain, grass, and woodlands of the entire Middle East. Wild foods may be eaten raw, boiled, baked or ground to flour. Of course, proper identification is imperative. It must be noted that poisons are interspersed as a natural defense mechanism to all growth. The reader must therefore take the following steps to correctly identify a wild edible plant.

RULES FOR POSITIVE IDENTIFICATION AND CONSUMPTION OF EDIBLE PLANTS

* Never collect edible plants closer than 100 feet from a road or inhabited areas.
* Never collect from areas treated with herbicides, pesticides, or other chemicals.
* Use three drawings or graphic references.
* Crush, sniff and inspect carefully.
* Rub a tiny bit on your gums and wait 20 minutes.
* Look for burning, nausea, itching, or stinging.
* If no untoward reaction, take a tiny bite and chew, spitting the plant out. Wait 20 minutes.
* Make a weak tea to further test edibility, waiting 20 minutes to test effects.
* Avoid burning plants as smoke may irritate.
* Teach children thoroughly.

AND FURTHER
* Eat only plant parts specified as *edible*.
* Red stems may indicate high levels of nitrate, which is poisonous to humans. Avoid red stems; eat green stems only.
* Because flowers are seasonal, they may not be in bloom to assist in identification.
* Safety from bacterial pollution may be a factor for any plant that grows in water. When in doubt, use purification tablets, if available, in washing plants.
* Dried large plants and whole branches of edible trees can be stored in warm, dry places.
* If possible, store small dried plants and seeds in glass.
* Roots hold a storehouse of nutrition and usually can be stored indefinitely in paper bags in warm, dry areas, then reconstituted by simmering.
* The nutritional content of dried wild foods found intact in winter has been estimated to be about half its nutritional content when fresh. In addition, the dried food has lost

about 80 to 90 percent of its water content. Dried plants can still be eaten, but be aware of the diminished available nutrition and adjust quantity accordingly.

Through the author's experience, the wild foods may be enhanced by many different **spices**, **additives**, and **supplements**. To list a few:

Butter or margarine, Kurdish *kara* or *kari*, Arabic *zubdah* or *samn sinagi*
Cardamon, Kurdish *hil*, Arabic *habelhal*
Cheese (soft), Kurdish *papka* or *tulaka*, Arabic *jibn akkaioi*
Cheese (sweet), Kurdish *panira shrin*, Arabic *jibn helou*
Cheese, Kurdish *panir*, Arabic *jibn ashawan*
Cinnamon, Kurdish *dârchini*, Arabic *qirfah*
Cumin, Kurdish *zira*, Arabic *kumun*
Fennel, *foeniculum vulgare*, Kurdish *razla* or *râzyâna*, Arabic *shumarah*
Ghee (purified butter grease), Kurdish *rowan*, Arabic *samnhamawi*
Ginger root, *officinalr*, Kurdish *zanjafil*, Arabic *zangabil* or *zingiber*
Lard (softened fat), Kurdish *chawri*, *baz*, *dûg* or *dûng*, Arabic *shahm*
Olive oil, Kurdish *tâma zaytûn*, Arabic *zayt zaytun*
Pepper, *piper*, Kurdish *âlat* or *filfil*, Arabic *fulful aswad*
Thyme, *thymus*, Kurdish *marza*, Arabic *za tar farisi*
Vegetable oil, Kurdish *rowana nibâti*, Arabic *zait nabati*
Watercress, *nosturtium officinale*, Kurdish *sheng*, Arabic *rashad*

[NOTICE: Since identification and use of wild plants requires particular care and attention, the author and publisher assume no responsibility whatsoever for any adverse effects encountered by individuals.]

ALOE VERA

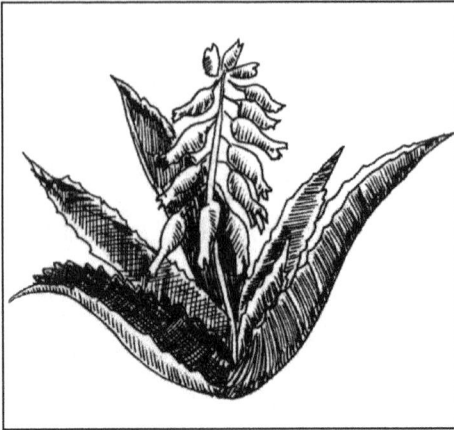

Aloe species
Drawing: *Aloe perfoliata*
also: *Aloe rubroviolaceae,
Aloe tomentoso*, Aloe perry[1]
Alias: *Medicinal Aloe,
Barbados Aloe*

WARNING: DO NOT USE AS BULK FOOD. USE SPARINGLY FOR MEDICINAL PURPOSES.

<u>Edible</u>: Leaves, flowers.

<u>Habitat</u>: Sandy, rocky soil.

<u>Distribution</u>: Noted in: Cliffs of Asir Mountains (orange flowers); on top of Jebel Feeba (hairy yellow flowers).

<u>Characteristics</u>: Green succulent leaves (called spikes) are filled with clear gel liquid. Mature plant has spikes up to 3' high with dense, arrow-shaped clusters of yellow (*aloe tomentoso*) or orange (*aloe rubroviolaceae*) flowers.

<u>Uses</u>: <u>Leaves</u>: *Internally*: In tea as an antispasmodic antihistamine (asthma, colds, congestion); anodyne; tranquilizer; diuretic. *Externally*: Crush leaves and apply gel as poultice for burns, sores. Promotes growth of new tissue. Antibiotic qualities. <u>Flowers</u>: Eat raw. Succulent.

<u>Hints</u>: For external use, slice leaf in half and place directly where needed. For internal use, remove gel and place in water. Refrigerate.

---

[1]Hooper, David. *Useful Plants and Drugs of Iran and Iraq*. Field Museum of Natural History. Chicago, June 30, 1937

ALOE VERA ICE CUBES

Place aloe vera leaf on the flat side and skim the skin off with a sharp knife. Scrape the gel with a spoon, holding on to end of leaf. Pour into ice cube trays and freeze.

ALOE VERA MORNING TONIC

Ingredients:
1 aloe vera ice cube
6 ounces freshly squeezed orange juice

Pour orange juice into glass. Add aloe vera ice cube. Drink tonic when cube has defrosted.

HINT: Substitute any fruit juice.

ALOE VERA FLOWERS

Eat flowers raw and add to favorite sandwiches, salads. Dip flowers in favorite sauces.

AMARANTH (Green amaranth)

Amaranthus species: *Amaranthus retroflexus*
Drawing: *Amaranthus, Amaranthus viridis*
Alias: *Pigweed, Red Root, Carelessweed*

Edible: Entire plant.

Habitat: Cultivated soils, oases.

Distribution: Entire Middle East. Noted in: Iran, Iraq, Jordan, Kurdistan[2], Turkey.

Characteristics: Height: 2'-6" or more. Bristly seed heads clustered on multi-branch stems from central stalk. Seeds are black and shiny. Leaves smooth and veined with slightly toothed margins.

Uses: High in vegetable protein. **Leaves:** Like spinach. Eat raw, steam, sauté; drink liquid used for cooking. Dry and grind for flour. Freezes well. **Seeds:** Winnow if desired. Use raw or dried for baking, cereal, mush. **Entire plant:** Steam, boil, use in soups and stews; drink liquid used for cooking. Include roots as rich source of extra nutrition.

Hints: Wait until amaranth is full grown for largest amount of seed heads. Harvest lower leaves and branches for vegetables.

---

[2]Holm, Leroy G., Herberger, T. P., Plucknett, D. L., *A Geographical Atlas of World Weeds.* NY: John Wiley & Sons, 1979

Use in simple soups, sandwiches, raw or cooked. Dry and powder to add green flour to bread mixes.

AMARANTH WILD MUFFINS

Ingredients:
1¾ cups amaranth flour
¼ cup olive oil OR sunflower oil
¾ cup water
½ cup raisins (optional)
1 teaspoon pure vanilla
2 teaspoons baking powder

Place amaranth flour in large mixing bowl. Add remaining ingredients. Mix well into a paste. Add to muffin cups, filling them ½ full. Bake at 350° for 20-25 minutes until golden brown. Let cool and remove from muffin tin.

AMARANTH WILD COOKIES

Drop spoonfuls of the paste onto a greased baking sheet. Bake at 350° for 20-25 minutes until golden brown.

WILD AMARANTH VEGETABLE BREAD

Ingredients:
2 1/4 cups package of active dry yeast
OR
2 3/5 ounce cakes of yeast
6 cups all purpose flour OR 10 cups whole wheat flour
1 1/2 cups tepid water
4 cups cooked, drained and chopped amaranth greens

Dissolve yeast according to package directions. Mix with flour. Add chopped greens and mix by hand. Let rise 1 hour and bake in preheated 400° oven about 40 minutes. Serve hot with a main meal. Loaves freeze well.

CATTAIL

Typha species
Drawing: *Typha*
also: *Typha domingensis, Typha augustata*
Alias: *Supermarket of the Swamp.*

WARNING: IF WATER PURITY IS IN DOUBT, USE PURIFICATION TABLET AND SOAK PLANT IN SOLUTION.

Edible: Roots, early shoots, stem pith, heads, pollen.

Habitat: Ditches with waste water, oases.

Distribution: Warm, temperate and tropical regions of the entire Middle East.

Characteristics: Grows in wet areas. Height: 3' high or more. Stalks have hot dog-shaped heads. Pollen flag in early spring. Very tall, slender leaves with one vein.

Uses: Plant holds about 30% complex carbohydrates; highly nutritious. **Roots:** Dry and grind for flour. **Early shoots:** Eat raw. Freeze. **Stem pith:** Peel stem, shell out pith. Eat raw, boil, pickle, freeze. **Early green heads:** Eat raw, cut and cook as ear of corn. **Early brown heads:** Grind for flour. **Pollen:** Use as nutrient additive.

Hints: Gather fluff from mature heads for excellent insulation or stuffing for jackets, etc. Fluff floats and is waterproof. Excellent tinder and torch. Use as cotton.

CATTAIL PITH CASSEROLE

Ingredients:
4 cups cattail piths 2" to 3" long (collected fresh and washed)
1 onion chopped OR 1 cup chives
Water to cover

Mix all ingredients. Pour into a greased casserole dish and bake at 350° for ½ hour. Top with favorite bread crumbs or sauce. Serves 6.

CATTAIL CORN ON THE COB

Ingredients:
Early green cattail heads (2-3 per person)
Boiling water to cover
Safflower oil, olive oil, or butter

Early in the season, harvest heads of cattails when the pollen spike is still green. Cut, leaving 2" of stem to hold the cob with. Pop the heads in boiling water and boil for 7 minutes. Remove and add oil or butter. Eat as you would corn on the cob. Highly nutritious.

CHICKWEED

Stellaria species
Drawing: *Stellaria media*
syn. *Alsine media*
Alias: *Common Chickweed, Starwort*

<u>Edible</u>: Entire plant.

<u>Habitat</u>: Sheltered cultivated ground, winter weed.

<u>Distribution</u>: Widespread in all temperate regions of Middle East. Noted in: marsh areas of Iran, Iraq, Kurdistan and Turkey.

<u>Characteristics</u>: Annual. Height: 1" or more. Creeps on ground; mats in gardens. Tiny paired opposite leaves. Starlike white flowers have five pairs of petals.

<u>Uses</u>: Highly nutritious. <u>Entire plant</u>: Eat raw, steam, boil, sauté; drink liquid used for cooking. Freezes well. Dry and powder for nutrient additive.

<u>Hint</u>: Chew stem for a lasting, milky gum.

CHICKWEED SALAD

Ingredients:
1 clove garlic
1 quart loosely packaged chickweed, washed
2 eggs, hard-cooked
4 tablespoons favorite dressing

Peel clove of garlic and rub wooden salad bowl. Chop chickweed finely. Add to salad bowl. Peel eggs, slice thin and add to bowl. Toss together with favorite salad dressing. Serves 4.

CHICKWEED A LA MEDITERRANEAN

Ingredients:
1 handful of washed chickweed plant (about 2 cups)
2 tablespoons olive oil
1 clove garlic, chopped finely
1 teaspoon thyme

Heat frying pan and add olive oil and chopped garlic. Brown garlic and add washed chickweed. Stir until piping hot.

VEGETABLE PROTEIN HAMBURGER

Ingredients:
1 cup cooked chickweed
½ cup falafil mix
Water

Chop cooked chickweed as finely as possible. Add falafil mix to it, combining and adding water a bit at a time until a claylike mixture results. Form into patties and fry slowly in a frying pan, turning when brown. A protein treat!

CRABGRASS

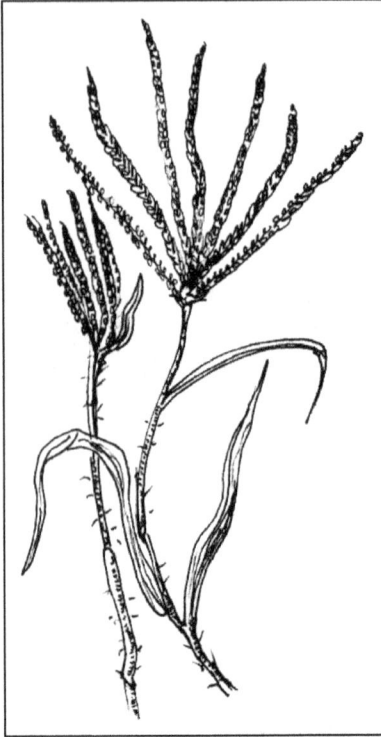

Gramineae species
Drawing: *Digitaria sangualis*
syn. *Panicum sanguinale*

WARNING: WHEN CUTTING GRASS-ES, LOOK OUT FOR BLACK DOTS (OR MOLD) BETWEEN SEEDS OR ON SHAFT. DO NOT USE THESE!

Edible: Seeds, stems.

Habitat: Open desert, dry ground.

Distribution: Around sand dunes, desert and cities. Temperate zones of entire Middle East. Noted in: Iran, Iraq, Kurdistan, Central Asia, Turkey.

Characteristics: Annual. 1' to 4' high.

Uses: Seeds: Eat raw. Dry and grind for flour. Stems: Use raw or dried for cereal, mush. Dry and grind for flour.

Hint: Store dried seeds in cardboard or glass, not plastic.

CRABGRASS CRACKERS (as per Wanda Wilde)

Ingredients:
1 cup favorite Basic Mix (see next)
1 cup crabgrass flour
½ cup water

Preheat oven to 400°. Lightly grease a baking sheet. In a medium-sized bowl, combine Basic Mix and flour. Add water to form dough. Knead about 12 times, until dough is smooth. Shape into pencil-like strands ½" thick or roll out flat onto baking sheet. Bake about 5 minutes until crisp. Cut into small pieces while still warm.

Variations: In place of crabgrass flour use any flour you have, such as malva neglecta, mixed grain, amaranth or lamb's quarters. Use goat's milk or regular milk in place of water.

BASIC MIX

Ingredients:
4¼ cups whole wheat flour
4¼ cups crabgrass flour
5 teaspoons baking powder
2 teaspoons cream of tartar
1½ cups instant dried regular milk OR dried goat's milk
1 teaspoon baking soda (optional)
1½ cups olive or peanut oil

In a large bowl, sift together flours, baking powder, cream of tartar, dried milk and baking soda. Blend well. With pastry blender, cut in oil until evenly distributed. Mixture will be only slightly damp. Put in large, airtight container. Label and store in a cool, dry place. Use within 10-12 weeks. Makes 13 cups.

CAKES

Crabgrass flour may be pressed together with just water. Pressed cakes are easily fried in oil.

DAISY

Crysanthemum species
Drawing: *Crysanthemum leucanthemum*
Alias: *Oxeye Daisy*

Note: LEAVE YELLOW CENTERS. EAT ONLY WHITE PETALS.

Edible: White petals, leaves and stems.

Habitat: Fields, valleys, most of Middle East.

Distribution: Wadis during cool rainy season.

Characteristics: Height: May reach 2' or more. White, rayed flower petals around pebbly yellow head. Erect single stem with alternate, narrow leaves that are clefted and deeply scalloped.

Uses: White petals: Eat raw in salads, sandwiches. Leaves and Stems: Eat raw as a vegetable or salad.

DAISY PETAL SALAD

Pick a quart of daisy petals and add your favorite dressing
OR
Place petals in pita sandwiches with favorite garnish.

DAISY LEAVES A LA MEDITERRANEAN

Ingredients:
1 handful of washed daisy leaves (about 2 cups)
2 tablespoons olive oil
1 clove garlic, chopped finely
1 teaspoon thyme

Heat frying pan and add olive oil and chopped garlic. Brown garlic and add washed daisy leaves. Stir until piping hot.

FILARIE, Redstem

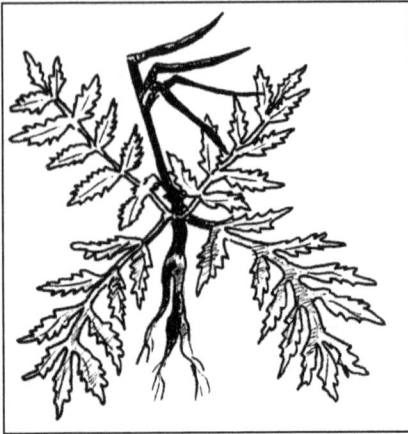

Erodium species
Drawing: *Erodium circularium (L'Her)* also: *Erodium cicinium, Erodium malaccides*
Alias: *Filarie, Alfilaree, Afilaria, Wild Celery, Stork's Bill*

WARNING: DO NOT INGEST FLOWERS OR STORK'S BILL FRUITS, AS THEY ARE KNOWN TO BE TOXIC. IT IS GENERALLY SAFE TO INGEST A LARGE AMOUNT OF LEAVES IF THE VEIN IN THE CENTER OF THE LEAF IS NOT PINK OR RED. FILARIE TENDS TO PICK UP NITRATES.

<u>Edible</u>: Leaves, roots.

<u>Habitat</u>: Dry areas, desert areas, claylike soils.

<u>Distribution</u>: Entire Middle East. Noted in: Cyprus, Egypt, Iran, Iraq, Jordan, in particular the lowland boarders of Kurdistan, Syria, and Turkey.

<u>Characteristics</u>: Dark green annual, winter annual, or biennial, reproducing from seeds at base of stork's bill-shaped roots. Flowers on long stalks shoot up from fernlike leaves lying in thick mats stemming from a central base. Stems hairy. Stalks have purple flowers, then seed buds. Stork's bill-shaped fruits have a seed that has a corkscrew tail, driving the seed into the hardest of soils. Flowers in March, April.

<u>Uses</u>: <u>Fernlike leaves:</u> Eaten raw, like celery. Use raw in soups, stews, sandwiches. <u>Leaves:</u> Steam and eat as a vegetable, or freeze. <u>Roots:</u> Eat raw like celery.

<u>Hint</u>: The seeds attached to their cork-screw tails bunch up for easy transporting to another area for replanting.

FILARIE SOUP

Ingredients:
1 large filarie head, minus buds and flowers
1 onion, thinly sliced
1 small potato, peeled and diced
Water to cover

Wash filarie head well, pulling out buds, flowers, and stork's bill fruits. Scrub root with a toothbrush. Place in pot and cover with water. Add onion and potato, cook on high heat for 1½ hours. Serve hot! Serves. 4.

FILARIE SANDWICH

Ingredients:
1 handful filarie leaves (no red stems, please)
2 slices whole wheat bread OR pita bread
Dash of your favorite spice
Dash of your favorite oil
Dash of your favorite vinegar
1 thinly sliced ring Bermuda onion (optional)

Additions: Layer all ingredients on a slice of whole wheat bread and enjoy a desert sandwich.

LAMB'S QUARTERS

Chenopodium species
Drawing: *Chenopodium album*
Alias: *Goosefoot, Wild Spinach, Pig Weed*
WARNING: PLANT LEAF RESEMBLES POISONOUS, MALODOROUS LOOK-ALIKE NETTLE LEAF GOOSEFOOT, WHICH SMELLS VERY BAD. IDENTIFY LAMB'S QUARTERS BY SMELL.

Edible: Entire plant.

Habitat: Cultivated ground.

Distribution: Widespread in Europe, North Africa and Asia, naturalized in temperate regions throughout world.

Characteristics: Height: 18" or more. Leaf shaped like goose foot, dark green with whitish underleaf. New leaves have white or lavender-tinged powder near center whorl. Leaf beads of water when wet. Green seedlike flower clusters.

Uses: High in nutrition, vitamins, calcium. Young roots: Boil, drink water used for cooking. Leaves: Like spinach. Eat raw, steam, boil, sauté; drink liquid used for cooking. Freeze. Dry and grind for flour. Flowers/seeds: Mush, cereal. Sprout. Dry and grind for flour.

Hint: Roots can be used as a soap substitute—wet hands and rub cleaned roots.

LAMB'S QUARTERS (*CHENOPODIUM ALBUM*) FACTS:
(Silver Leaf Spinach, Goosefoot, Pigweed, Lamb's Quarters)

* 2 cups equals 14,000-16,000 units of vitamin A. Adults need about 5,000 units of vitamin A a day.
* 2 cups equals 66-130 milligrams of vitamin C. Adults need 70 milligrams of vitamin C a day.

* Lamb's quarters provide one of the highest fiber contents of any grown vegetable.

Pick a bundle of lamb's quarters. Hang upside down in a warm area to dry. Lay a sheet on the floor. Strip off all leaves and seeds and then dry thoroughly and "crunch." Put leaves and seeds through a hand grinder for instant green nutritious flour, to be used in all recipes calling for flour: ¼ cup vegetable flour for each 1 cup of regular flour. Work your way to full strength. Author just uses water and makes a pancake the size of a silver dollar and fries lightly, using olive oil.

LAMB'S QUARTERS TOPS

Fill your favorite pot with tops, leaves and seeds. Cover with water. Simmer 7 minutes. Drain, and add your favorite seasoning. Serve hot.

BROWN RICE AND LAMB'S QUARTER SPROUTS

Ingredients:
1 cup lamb's quarter sprouts (sprout seeds only 1½ to 2 days)
2 tablespoons corn oil OR peanut oil
1 tablespoon chopped scallions OR chives OR onions
¼ cup thin-sliced canned OR fresh mushrooms
1 tablespoon soy sauce OR favorite garnish
1 cup cooked brown rice

Heat oil in heavy fry pan or wok. Add onion, mushrooms. Stir-fry until lightly brown. Add soy sauce, rice and sprouts. Stir-fry for 3 to 4 minutes. Cover and simmer for 5 more minutes. Serves 3 to 4.

MALVA NEGLECTA

Mallow species
Drawing: *Malva neglecta*
Alias: *Cheeses*

Edible: Tender young leaves, seeds.

Habitat: Abundant in sandy deserts, waste and culti-vated soils.

Distribution: Most of Middle East. Noted in: Aegean Islands, Bahrain, Cyprus, Dubai, Egypt, Iran, Iraq, Jordan, restricted to border areas of Kurdistan facing Mesopotamia lowlands, Pakistan, Palestine, Saudi Arabia, Sinai, Syria, and Turkey.

Characteristics: Annual. Many species. Height: 4" or more; mature plant may reach 14" or more. Leaves are circular and shallow-lobed. Seeds are cheese-shaped discs. White, pink, or lavender five-petaled flowers; notch at end of each petal. Increases saliva flow. Lubricates mouth and throat.

Uses: Young leaves: Eat raw, steam, boil, sauté; drink liquid used for cooking. Freeze. Dry and powder for flour or nutrient additive. High in iron and calcium. Roots: Raw.

Hints: Mince mallow leaf and marinate in oil and vinegar before cooking. Eat only a cup at a time (so high in iron and calcium it may give a feeling of fullness quickly).

DELICATE WILD MALVA SOUP

Ingredients:
1 handful of washed malva neglecta leaves
2 cups water
2 small onions, sliced thin
¼ cup malva neglecta "cheeses" or seeds

Place soup pot on medium heat. Place malva neglecta leaves in two cups of water. Allow to come to a boil. Turn off heat, stir leaves and cover. Steep soup for 10 minutes, remove leaves if desired, add onion slices and "cheeses." Serve hot. Serves 2.

WILD MALVA RICE CASSEROLE

Ingredients:
1 cup water
12 large malva neglecta leaves
1 cup cooked wild rice
½ teaspoon thyme
½ teaspoon vegetable salt (of your choice)
Small casserole dish, greased

Bring water to a boil. Wilt mallows by gingerly dipping each leaf separately into boiling water. Rearrange leaf on a paper towel to drain. Place wild rice in a bowl. Stir in thyme and ¼ teaspoon vegetable salt. Take a teaspoon of mixture and place in the middle of the leaf. Roll the leaf and mixture up to the stem, then tuck stem in to secure. Place whole roll-up face down in casserole dish. Sprinkle rest of vegetable salt over roll-ups and bake in oven for 20 minutes at 350°. Serve piping hot. Makes one dozen, serves 2 people.

MUSTARD (Wild Mustard)

Herraisha, Tournefortii
Brassica species
Drawing: *Brassica*
Alias: *Charlock Mustard*

Edible: Stems, leaves, flowers, seeds.

Habitat: Roadsides, cultivated lands and desert sandy soils.

Distribution: Most of Middle East. Noted in: Lower elevation valleys of Kurdistan, Mediterranean to Baluchistan.

Characteristics: Height: 10" or more. Leaves rounded, with one or two extra protuberances of tiny leaves below main part of leaf. Crushed leaf yields herby, pungent smell. Four-petaled yellow flower; petals in form of cross. Black seeds in pod. Mustard is a very pungent potherb.

Uses: Stems: Use raw as pungent spice. Leaves: Eat raw, use as pungent spice, steam, boil in soups, stews. Flowers: Eat raw, steam. Freeze or dry. Seeds: Dry and use as spice; grind for mustard.

Hint: When eating a quantity of mustard leaves as a vegetable, boil in water 30 minutes.

MUSTARD FLOWER "WILD BROCCOLI"

Ingredients:
4 cups mustard buds (pulled off stems)
1 quart boiling water
2 tablespoons olive oil

Wash buds thoroughly. Add to boiling water and simmer 5 minutes. Drain, add oil and serve.

MUSTARD GREENS

Ingredients:
1 quart young mustard leaves
1 clove garlic, chopped
1 teaspoon lemon juice
1 teaspoon vinegar
1 tablespoon olive oil

Boil leaves for 30 minutes. Drain. Add remaining ingredients and serve hot.

NUTSEDGE

Cyperus Rodundus species
Drawing: *Cyperaceae*
Alias: *Chufa*
WARNING: WHEN CUTTING GRASSES, LOOK OUT FOR BLACK DOTS (OR MOLD) BETWEEN SEEDS OR ON SHAFT. DO NOT USE THESE!

Edible: Seeds, stems.
Habitat: (Summer) damp, sandy soil.
Distribution: Entire Middle East.

Characteristics: Seed flowers yellow to reddish brown. 8" to 3'. Native, perennial.

Uses: Seeds, stems, leaves: dried and ground to flour; raw in cereal, mush. Roots/corms (nut-like extensions): Eat raw.
Hint: Pull carefully to keep "nuts" on ends of roots.

WILD OAT

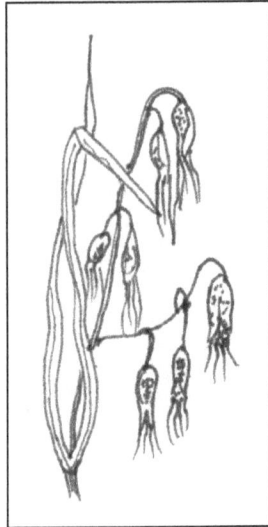

Gramineae species
Drawing: *Avena sterilis*
Edible: Seed head.
Habitat: Cultivated grounds.
Distribution: Most of Middle East. Noted in: Iran, Iraq, Kurdistan, Saudi Arabia and Turkey.

Characteristics: Annual. Stout grass, tufted seed carriers, leaf blades long, flat and rigid, rough on surfaces. Slightly hairy areas in joints.

Uses: Seeds, stems. Eat raw, in cereal, mush. Dry and grind for flour. **Hint:** Keep whole grass including stems in cardboard, glass or burlap. Keep dry for future flour.

NUTSEDGE OR WILD OAT FLOUR

Grind to flour when seeds are dry. Nutsedge flour has a nutty taste. Store in glass when possible, or store whole plants in bags, grinding when flour is used.

CRACKERS

Ingredients:
1 cup Basic Mix (pg 13)
1 cup nutsedge OR wild oat flour
½ cup water

Preheat oven to 400°. Lightly grease a baking sheet. In a medium-sized bowl, combine Basic Mix and flour. Add water to form dough. Knead about 12 times, until dough is smooth. Shape into pencil-like strands ½" thick or roll out flat onto baking sheet. Bake about 5 minutes until crisp. Cut into small pieces while warm.

Variations: Use any flour you have such as mallow, mixed grain or lamb's quarters in place of nutsedge or oat. Use goat's milk or regular milk in place of water.

PHRAGMITES

Phragmites species
Drawing: *Phragmites communis*
also: *Phragmites australis*
Alias: *Reed, Reedgrass*

WARNING: IF WATER PURITY IS IN DOUBT, USE PURIFICATION TABLET AND SOAK PLANT IN SOLUTION. RINSE AND BOIL PLANT 20 MINUTES.

WARNING: When cutting grasses look out for black dots (or mold) between seeds or on shaft. Do not use these!

Edible: Roots, stem pith, seed plumes.

Habitat: Frequent in ditches and wet ground.

Distribution: Widespread in temperate regions of the entire Middle East. Noted in: Iran, Southern Iraq, Southern Kurdistan, Saudi Arabia, and Turkey.

Characteristics: Perennials. Height: 2' or more. Wavy seed plumes. Jointed, hollow stems. Grows in brackish water.

Uses: Roots: Crush and pound for flour. Stem pith: Simmer for nutrition. Seed plumes: Use for cereal, gruel, flour.

Hints: Weave stems for mats, bedding, thatching, grass huts. Excellent tinder.

PHRAGMITES PITA CAKE

Ingredients:
1 cup phragmites flour
1 cup whole wheat flour
¼ cup olive oil
1 tablespoon baking powder
Water

Add all ingredients to a large bowl. Mix slowly, adding water a little at a time until you have a mix. Knead and let sit for 10 minutes, covered. Pat clay-like patties onto a greased baking sheet. Bake at 350° until the edge of pita breads are brown and crispy.

PHRAGMITES COOKIES

Ingredients:
1 cup phragmites
1 cup bran fiber flour OR 1 cup whole wheat flour
2 tablespoons safflower oil
Water to make paste

Blend ingredients and spoon onto baking sheets (silver dollar size is perfect). Bake at 350° for 10-15 minutes until crispy. Delicious! Some people prefer to add ½ cup honey to recipe.

PLANTAIN

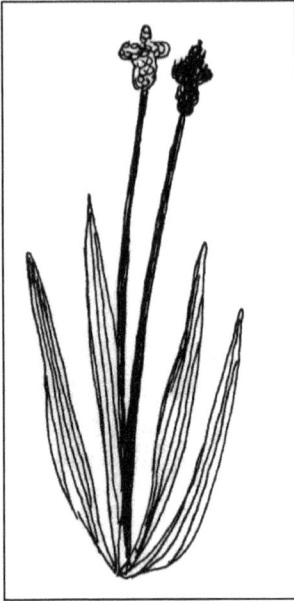

Plantago species
Drawing: *Plantago lanceolata* (narrow leafed)
also: *Plantago major* (broad leafed)
Alias: *Soldier's Herb, Ribwort*

<u>Edible</u>: Entire plant.

<u>Habitat:</u> Gardens, orchards, lawn and desert oases.

<u>Distribution:</u> Most of Middle East. Noted in: Afghanistan, Bahrain, Cyprus, Egypt, Iran, Iraq, Jordan, Kurdistan, Pakistan, Palestine, Saudi Arabia, Syria, and Turkey[3].

<u>Characteristics</u>: Annual. Two types: short, broad leaf, 2" to 8"; long narrow leaf, 10" or longer. Both types of leaves heavy-veined. Both types have center spikes with seeds. *Plantago ovata*, desert type, has furry stems, leaves.

<u>Uses:</u> <u>Leaves:</u> Eat raw, steam, boil, sauté; drink liquid used for cooking. Use in soups and stews. Dry, freeze. <u>Seeds:</u> Run finger up spike to gather seeds. Use for baking, spice, sprouting. <u>Entire plant</u>: Steam, boil; drink liquid used for cooking. Use in soups and stews.

<u>Hint:</u> For an antiseptic bandage, "bruise" a plantain leaf and place on wound.

---

[3]Hooper, David. *Useful Plants and Drugs of Iran and Iraq.*Field Museum of Natural History. Chicago, June 30, 1937

WILD PLANTAIN COOKIES

Ingredients:
2 cups whole wheat flour
¾ cup plantain seeds (dried or fresh)
4 teaspoons baking powder
2 tablespoons molasses
½ cup (1 package) carob-covered raisins

Mix all ingredients well in a big bowl. Add tepid water slowly to form a thick, claylike paste. To form cookies, roll a pinch of dough between your palms and press onto a greased cookie sheet. Bake 15 minutes at 350° or until golden brown.

PLANTAIN SANDWICHES, SALADS

Add leaves raw to pita breads or salads. Stir fry seed heads or eat raw.

PURSLANE

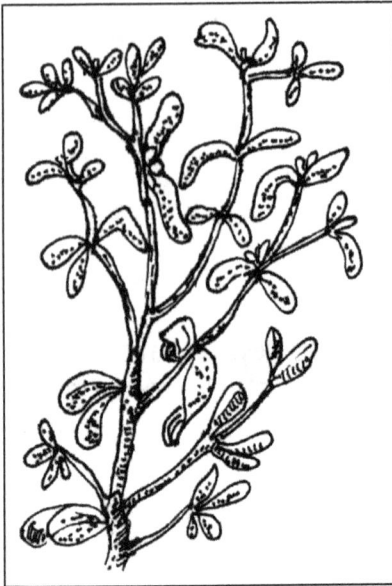

Portulaca species
Drawing: *Portulaca oleracea*
Alias: *Pussley, Pursley*

Edible: Entire plant.

Habitat: Abundant in abandoned fields, waste ground, gardens, cultivated and moist ground. Desert ground, oases.

Distribution: Warm, temperate regions of entire Middle East.

Characteristics: Annual. Height: 1" to 12" or more. Succulent. Flat-lobed rounded leaf, oval in shape. Creeps on ground; mats in gardens.

Uses: Highly nutritious. Stems: Pickle and store. Entire plant: Eat raw (large amounts may be eaten to quench thirst), steam, boil, sauté; drink liquid used for cooking. Freeze. Dry and powder for nutrient additive. Very high in vitamins and minerals.

Hints: Grows well indoors. Check saltiness (some plants pull up easier than others).

PURSLANE SALAD

Ingredients:
1 clove garlic
2 cups purslane
1 onion, thinly sliced
2 tablespoons favorite salad dressing. (Author prefers oil and herbal vinegar.)
Wooden bowl

Take clove of garlic and rub wooden bowl thoroughly. Discard garlic. Add remaining ingredients to bowl and toss lightly.

PURSLANE SANDWICH

Pick young leaves and wash thoroughly. Use as lettuce in a pita bread sandwich. Enjoy!

PURSLANE VEGETABLE

Ingredients:
4 cups purslane, washed and drained
1 egg beaten OR ½ cup okra stew
½ cup finely ground breadcrumbs
1 teaspoon peanut oil OR olive oil

Finely chop 4 cups purslane, stems and all. Add egg or okra stew and breadcrumbs. Turn into a baking dish well greased with oil and add your favorite seasoning. Bake at 325° for 20 minutes, until piping hot. Serves 4.

SORREL

Oxalidaceae species
Drawing: *Oxalis corniculata*
Alias: *Lemon grass, Shamrock clover*

WARNING: CAUTION. *SORREL* IN RAW STATE WILL CAUSE OXALIC ACID CRYSTALS TO STORE IN THE BODY. THIS WILL CAUSE THE ELIMINATION OF CALCIUM AND INHIBIT THE ABSORPTION OF CALCIUM. DO NOT EAT RAW.

COOK FOR SAFETY AND VITAMIN C CONTENT.

<u>Edible</u>: Entire plant, COOKED.

<u>Habitat</u>: Fields, woods, moist places under lawn trees, shrubs.

<u>Distribution</u>: Widespread in the entire Middle East.

<u>Characteristics</u>: Annual herb reproducing by seed. Leaves are divided into 3 heart-shaped leaflets (like a shamrock), sour lemon taste. Grows from 2" to 8" in bunches, carpets. Sometimes has a hairy, soft down, rooting at the joints. Flowers 7-11 mm long, with 5 yellow, rarely green petals. Sometimes red at the base. Leaves fold up sometimes in extremely warm sunshine.

<u>Uses</u>: Leaves: Use in soups, stews. Seeds: Use in soups, stews. Flowers: Use in soups, stews.

<u>Hint</u>: All sorrels are antiseptic; wash for skin eruptions.

GREENS SOUP

Ingredients:
1 cup fresh sorrel leaves, flowers, stems
1 onion, thinly sliced
Water to cover

Place sorrel in a pot and cover with water. Add onion and simmer for a few minutes. Leaves will turn from bright green to olive green. This is normal and insures the oxalic acid crystals are destroyed. Serve hot. Delicious!

CREAMED SORREL SOUP

Ingredients:
4 cups of sorrel leaves, washed
2 teaspoons of safflower oil OR olive oil
2 teaspoons wheat germ
1 onion, chopped
4 cups non-fat dried milk OR goat's milk
OR
4 cups water (Author prefers)

Place leaves in pot, cover with water and simmer slowly for ½ hour. Blend in remaining ingredients, simmer and strain. Serves 4.

SOW THISTLE

Compositae species
Drawing: *Sonchus oleraceus*
Alias: *Pig's ear*

<u>Edible</u>: Entire plant.

Habitat: Abundant in gardens, orchards, fields, moist ground, sandy deserts.

Distribution: Native of "Old World" cool, temperate regions. Naturalized in "New World." Most of Middle East.

Characteristics: Basal leaves deeply serrated. Dandelion-type, deeply lobed leaves begin from a central stem on the ground. Center stalk bears a leaf that clasps around the stalk and goes to a sharp point, like a sow's "ear." Top of stalk bears branches. At the end of each grows a yellow flower that looks somewhat like a dandelion flower. After seeding, a white fuzz appears with single seeds on the end of the fluff.

Uses: <u>Young</u> <u>leaves</u>: Nutritious raw as spring green. Use in soups, casseroles. <u>Flower</u>: Eaten raw, stir-fry; dry, freeze. <u>Roots</u>: Raw or cooked.

<u>Hint</u>: Remove buds on end of stalks. Place in paper bag or glass. Buds continue to mature and burst open with fluff. On the end of each "parachute" is a single seed for replanting. (Children love this process.)

WILD SOW THISTLE STIR-FRY

Ingredients:
1 cup wild sow thistle leaves
½ cup wild sow thistle buds and flowers
½ cup red cabbage
1 clove garlic, pressed
1 teaspoon wild thyme
3 tablespoons oil and vinegar

Combine all ingredients in a salad bowl, toss gently and serve.

VEGETARIAN BURGER

Ingredients:
2 cups cooked lentils
½ onion, peeled
2 tablespoons sow thistle leaves, steamed and chopped

Combine all ingredients and mix until everything sticks together. Makes 6 medium-sized burgers.

SOW THISTLE SOUP

Ingredients:
1 cup sow thistle tips
1 clove garlic
1 onion, thinly sliced
Water to cover

Place sow thistle tips in water to cover. Simmer for 20 minutes on low heat. (Slow cooker is excellent; simmer for 1 hour on low.) Add garlic, onion, and serve hot.

WARNING! WARNING!

The following plants are poisonous and *MUST NOT* be eaten.
They are included here to warn the reader against using them.

BINDWEED - POISON

Convolvulus arvensis species
Drawing: *Convolvulus arvensis*
Alias: *Morning Glory*

NON-EDIBLE POISON.

WARNING: POISON. DO NOT INGEST ANY PART OF THIS PLANT.

Habitat: Abundant in road-sides, gardens, waste ground.

Distribution: Temperate regions of the entire Middle East.

Characteristics: Perennial. Twisting, trailing herb, creeping rootstock, white and pinkish trumpetlike flowers. Arrow-shaped leaves.

BLACK NIGHTSHADE - POISON

Solanaceae, Solanum species
Drawing: *Solanum nigrum*
Alias: *Ground Cherries*

NON-EDIBLE POISON.

WARNING: POISON. DO NOT INGEST ANY PART OF THIS DANGEROUS PLANT.

Habitat: Frequent in waste ground.

Distribution: Cosmopolitan. Entire Middle East.

Characteristics: Annual herb. 6" to 2" high. Stems have many branches, fruit is green when young, round and black when mature.

JINSON WEED - POISON

Solanaceae, Datura species
Drawing: *Datura innoxia*
Alias: *Trumpet weed, Thorn apple*

NON-EDIBLE POISON.

WARNING: POISON. DO NOT INGEST ANY PART OF THIS DANGEROUS PLANT.

Habitat: Cultivated and moist ground.

Distribution: Entire Middle East.

Characteristics: Trumpet-shaped white flower. Walnut-sized spiny burr. Grayish green soft downy leaves.

NOTES

REFERENCES

Al-Rawi, Ali. *Flora of Kuwait*. Volume Two: *Compositae and Monoccotyledonae*. Safat, Kuwait: Kuwait University, Faculty of Science, P.O. Box 5969, Safat 13060, Kuwait, 1987.

Boulos, Loufly. *The Weed Flora of Kuwait*. Kuwait: Kuwait University, 1988.

Daoud, Hazim S., revised by Ali Al-Rawi. *Flora of Kuwait*. Volume One: *Dicotyledoneae*. London: KPI Limited; 14 Leichester Square, London, Wc2H 7PH, England, 1985.

Hooper, David. *Useful Plants and Drugs of Iran and Iraq*. Field Museum of Natural History. Chicago: June 30, 1937.

Holm, Leroy G.; Herberger, T. P.; Plucknett, D. L.; *A Geographical Atlas of World Weeds*. NY: John Wiley & Sons, 1979

Runyon, Linda. *A Survival Acre*; *The Essential Wild Food Survival Guide*; *Homestead Memories*; *Wild Food and Animals Coloring Book*; *Why Not Love?*; "Edible Wilds Food Card Deck" P.O. Box 83, Shiloh, NJ 08353. The Wild Food Company. www.OfTheField.com, lrunyon8@yahoo.com.

Vincett, Betty A. Lipscombe. *Golden Days in the Desert*: *Wild Flowers of Saudi Arabia*. Italy: Immel Publishing, 1984.

Vincett, Betty A. Lipscombe. *Wild Flowers of Central Saudi Arabia*. Milano, Italy: Pl. ME. Editrice, Milano, 1977.

Western, A.R., *The Flora of the United Arab Emirates: An Introduction*. United Arab Emirates University, 1989.

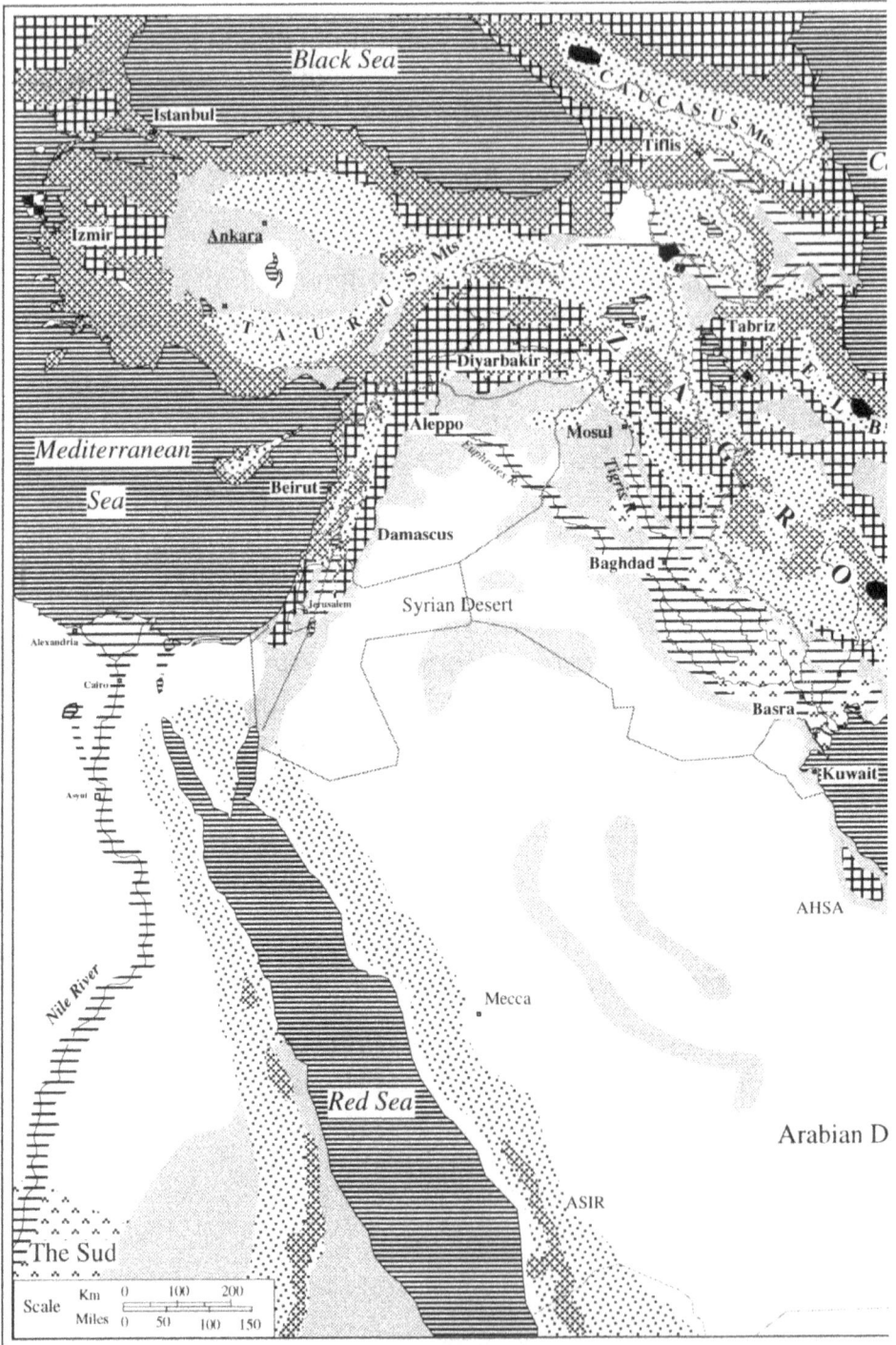

Black Sea

Istanbul

CAUCASUS Mts.

Tiflis

C

Izmir

Ankara

Tabriz

T A U R U S Mts.

Diyarbakir

Mediterranean

Aleppo

Mosul

Z A G R O

Sea

Beirut

Euphrates

Tigris

Damascus

Baghdad

Jerusalem

Syrian Desert

Alexandria

Cairo

Basra

Asyut

Kuwait

AHSA

Nile River

Mecca

Red Sea

Arabian D

ASIR

The Sud

Scale	Km	0	100	200	
	Miles	0	50	100	150

MAP OF THE MIDDLE EAST, FEBRUARY 1997 - Topography

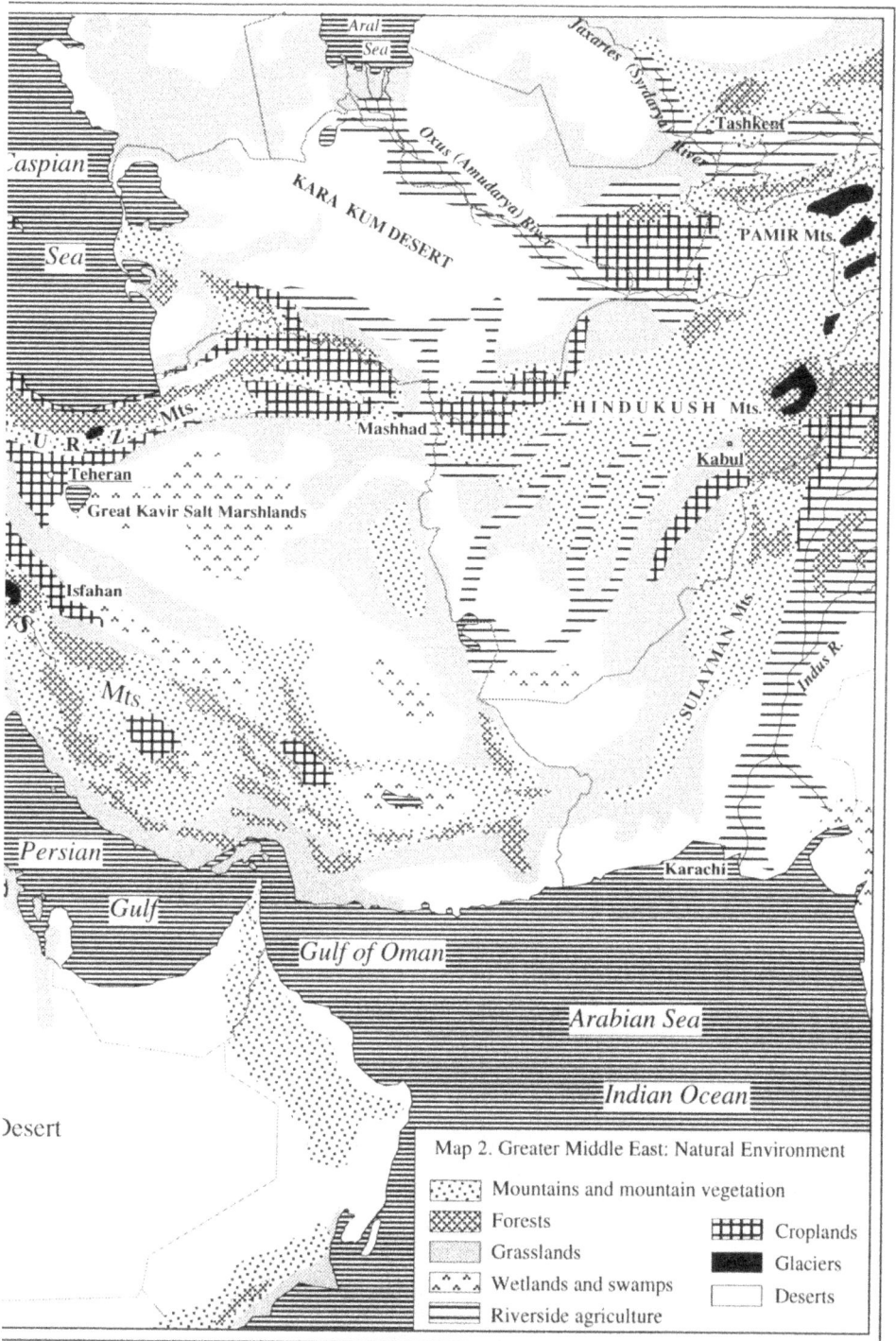

Map 2. Greater Middle East: Natural Environment

- Mountains and mountain vegetation
- Forests
- Grasslands
- Wetlands and swamps
- Riverside agriculture
- Croplands
- Glaciers
- Deserts

MAP OF THE MIDDLE EAST, FEBRUARY 1997 - Topography

www.ingramcontent.com/pod-product-compliance
Lightning Source LLC
Chambersburg PA
CBHW061756040426

42447CB00011B/2335